I GOES TO
FIGHT
MIT REBBE'N

HC HUBER

TABLE OF CONTENTS

Introduction 1

I. The Boat Sichah 4

II. The Tamar Sichah 7

III. The Journeys Sichah 9

IV. The Milk Sichah 15

V. The 'Korach' Sichah 18

VI. The Counting the Omer Sichah 20

VII. The Mixed Multitude and Golden Calf Sichah 25

VIII. The Eliezer Sichah 29

IX. The Miriam Sichah 32

X. The Avram Sichah 35

Conclusions and Personal Thoughts 39

Acknowledgement 43

INSPIRATIONAL QUOTES

May it be Your will ... that the temple be
speedily rebuilt in our days, and grant us
(and each of us) our portion in Your Torah.

—Pirke Avot 5:20

Only those who will risk going too far
can possibly find out how far one can go.

—T.S. Elliot

Elevate those guns a little lower.

—Andrew Jackson
(also, according to Shelby Foote,
Nathan Bedford Forrest)

I goes to fight mit Sigel.

—anonymous "Dutch" volunteer
in the Civil War

INTRODUCTION

This is a presentation of excerpts from Sichahs (writings of the Rebbe) about the interplay between personal Free Choice and Divine Providence. By Divine Providence, I mean that G-d controls events and outcomes, as opposed to events and outcomes being determined by fate, chance, or human choice. From a Jewish perspective, there is a well-known axiom that, "Everything is in the hands of heaven, except the fear of heaven." (Talmud, Brachos 33B). This statement tells us that G-d, indeed, runs our world, but there is an exception to this rule. In matters that involve whether to obey a commandment from G-d, people have free choice. In such a system, reward and punishment are perfectly understandable. If you obey G-d's commandments, you earn reward. If you transgress, you deserve punishment. As we will see, the Rebbe is going to force us to reevaluate this comfortable resolution of the conflict.

The focus of this work will be on ten of the Rebbe's Yiddish Sichahs as printed in Likkutei Sichot. The translations that follow are my own with no attempt at making a literal, word-for-word translation. I wanted to convey the ideas in simple, flowing English, hence, my designation as "free translation" for all the excerpts. There may be room for critique of the translations, however, I hope this does not become the focus. Rather, I would like to see any analysis and comments directed toward a better and more complete understanding of the ideas contained in the Rebbe's words. In case of real doubt, the Sichahs are there for everyone to read for themselves.

I also hope not to have this work dismissed by someone thinking, "Oh, Free Choice and Divine Providence; the Rambam (or some other earlier authority) explained that!" Such a statement would be true, but that is the point. The Rebbe was certainly familiar with anything of significance previously written on the subject. All this earlier material was understood by the Rebbe, as only the Rebbe could process it. With all prior sources as his foundation, the Rebbe wrote what he wrote.

The excerpts to be discussed were found over a period of time. Sometimes the footnotes of one Sichah lead to another Sichah on the subject. Others were encountered in a random manner. This collection is not meant to be exhaustive. I am sure there are other statements on this topic, from the Rebbe and the earlier Rebbeim of Chabad, that would contribute to a more complete understanding of the subject.

The format for this presentation is as follows: Each Sichah is given a label (i.e., The Boat Sichah, The Milk Sichah) for purpose of easy reference. Then follows, in my own words, a very brief description of the overall content of the Sichah, in order that the reader should have some idea of the context for the Rebbe's words. After that, will appear the designation "free translation" followed by my translation of the Rebbe's words. When this is completed, there will appear the phrase "end of the Rebbe's words." After that, I offer my explanation as to what I believe each particular excerpt adds to the overall discussion.

A brief word here on the subject itself. It is a conundrum how to reconcile Divine Providence and Free Choice existing side by side. Hence, it is not only difficult to grasp what the Rebbe is always saying, but it is also controversial. I recently saw in a Sichah (Vol. 17, page 263, bottom of second column) how one might deal with such a situation. In the Jerusalem Talmud, Sheviit, Chapter 8, law 5, the sages relate: Yehudah from Hutzie isolated himself in a cave for three days in the hope of understanding a teaching (related to giving charity) that he could not grasp. When this did not help, he inquired of Rebbe Yossi for an explanation …

There a plenty of caves in Missouri (where I live), but personally, they make me feel claustrophobic. If we had a Rebbe Yossi, it would make sense to seek an audience with him. Failing on both of these options, I have done my best to understand the concept, as explained by the Rebbe.

Finally, I am not a rabbi, or the spokesperson for anyone or any group. By profession, I am a lawyer that handles personal bankruptcies and fixes traffic tickets. As a result of these limitations, I want the words of the Rebbe to be the focus and not my comments on his words. As such, I have taken pains to keep my comments brief and muted, so as not to divert attention from the words of the Rebbe. Having said all this, I am optimistic that readers will be open-minded enough to consider a new or different opinion on this issue, and that people from a variety of backgrounds will be challenged and inspired.

I.
THE BOAT
SICHAH

Vol. 19, page 242, paragraph 11

CIRCA 1974

Chapter 28 of Deuteronomy contains the "Rebuke" for sins. The focus of the Sichah is on verse 68, and Rashi's comments on the verse. The words in parenthesis are my additions.

(Free translation) It is not just that the "Rebuke" was given to get people to do Teshuvah (repent). The truth is that even the underlying causes that made the "Rebuke" necessary, the sins, were for the purpose of getting people to ultimately do Teshuvah.

It appears to us that the exile is a result of the sins the people committed of their own free choice. However, the ultimate reality is that the exile was imposed from above. G-d brought the people to such a state in order that they should have the benefit that comes from doing Teshuvah. (This benefit is that through Teshuvah, "intentional sins" are transformed into "merits"; paragraph 12 of this Sichah).

This is hinted at in the words of the verse, "and G-d will cause you to return ... in the way I told you never to look upon again." This means, the people will sin, and do things that are explicitly forbidden by G-d. Nevertheless, this is ultimately directed and orchestrated from above. The point being, to ultimately elevate the people through their doing Teshuvah.

Therefore, Rashi explains "in boats," as "in captivity." The point being that the decent of an individual into boundaries, limitations, darkness, and concealment is not something the person chooses to do of his or her own free will. It is as if they were taken captive. It was G-d who forced them into the situation, with the intent to lead him or her to the benefit that can only be attained through Teshuvah. (End of the Rebbe's words).

This Sichah was my first exposure to how the Rebbe viewed the interplay between Free Choice and Divine Providence. This is one of the reasons for making this Sichah the first one to be discussed. I was taken aback by the Rebbe's assertion that G-d "forces" people to sin! G-d controls everything, even in our choices on whether to obey His commandments. The reason for this is to reap the benefit that comes from doing Teshuvah on intentional sins.

The Rebbe does speak of a "revealed" reality and an "inner" reality. However, it is not that the revealed reality is a sham and only the inner reality is actually true. In our revealed reality, the exile is a result of our sins committed with free choice. The Rebbe does not say, it only appears to us that our sins committed with free choice brought on the exile. This bolsters the reality of free choice. However, the Rebbe then bolsters the dominance of Divine Providence by saying that pursuant to the inner reality, the exile (and the sins which "caused" it) comes from above.

This is the point. I think the Rebbe wants us to realize that it is not one or the other. It is both. There is free choice, and there is the alternative of everything being in the hands of heaven. The Rebbe is not particularly concerned with explaining how this can be. He just wants us to know that both concepts are.

In footnote 49, the Rebbe references Toras Chaim, parshas Toldot, by the Mitteler Rebbe. In many of these Sichos, the Rebbe cites this as his primary source. It is a very long treatise comprised heavily of terse references to other sources, and in short, is way above my level of learning. Still, one can see that the Mitteler Rebbe goes back and forth between emphasizing the validity of the two realities we are dealing with. Perhaps it is fair to conclude that the Rebbe has condensed and summarized in the brief excerpt

I have quoted what the Mitteler Rebbe describes at such length. If nothing else, it is a testament to the Rebbe's ability to take the teachings of the earlier Rebbeim and make them relevant, meaningful, and instructive to "blue collar" students of his own generation.

On the other hand, perhaps we need not throw our hands up in complete resignation. In another place, the Rebbe speaks to the issue of reconciling conflicting concepts (Vol. 17, Likkutei Sichot, pages 307–09, paragraphs 6 and 7). The Rebbe says the apparent contradiction is a result of the "limitation of the creatures (meaning us humans) and the limitations of creation, as a whole. However, if one can find a way to address the issue with a mindset that is open to accepting everything as the will of G-d, then the contradiction falls away, since they are both expressions of G-d's will. Furthermore, from G-d's essential perspective, which can tolerate opposites, both concepts can co-exist at the same time!"

Perhaps this idea is contained in the Mishnah in Pirke Avot 2:4. We are exhorted to nullify our will to G-d's will. If we succeed in doing so, all opposing forces fall away and everything starts to make sense.

At this point I wanted to discuss the context of the discussion. That is, why the Rebbe chose to discuss it in connection with the Tochacha, the Rebuke, which is a prophecy about exile. Other references that follow are tied to specific events or mitzvahs. Exile, on the one hand, is a descent resulting from our sins. It is sometimes pinned on the Big Sins, like the Sin of the Tree of Knowledge, which implicates all of mankind, or the Sin of the Golden Calf, the everlasting scourge of the entire Jewish People. On the other hand, the sages and the prophets focus on specific sins of the generations leading up to the destruction of the temples. Again, on the one hand, exile is a descent caused by our sins committed with Free Choice. On the other hand, it is a result of events orchestrated from above, which are for the ultimate good. In the final analysis, both are true. So, while not minimizing the consequences of sin, we need not overreact with despair or anguish over events that are part of G-d's plan (even on Tishah B'Av). This applies when examining the Big Sins, as just mentioned, as well as individual sins, one's own or those of another.

II.

THE TAMAR SICHAH

Vol. 5, page 195, paragraph 11

CIRCA 1968

Chapter 38 of Genesis describes the relationship between Judah and Tamar, his daughter-in-law. The focus of the Sichah is on verse 26 which contains Judah's admission that he is the father of her unborn children.

(Free translation) This is how to understand the two opposing dynamics that were at play regarding the incident with Tamar. At first, we assumed that because of her "harlotry" she is ordered to be taken out to be punished. Afterward, we find out that at the very same instant, a "bas kol," a heavenly voice, declares, "from Me and from within Me all this happened!" Why all this drama? To bring forth kings and ultimately Mashiach and the Redemption. (End of the Rebbe's words).

In a footnote to this Sichah (footnote 80), the Rebbe tells us that it is "obvious" that G-d does not want sins for themselves. A sin is, by definition, an act in opposition to G-d's will, and will never be elevated. The statement that intentional sins become like merits through Teshuvah, is only referring to the spark of holiness that fell into the sins, and not the sins themselves.

The Rebbe labels the two elements that are present here as "two opposing dynamics." There is Tamar making decisions and taking actions based on her own free choice, and at the same time, G-d declares that "it all came from me!" The rational mind says, "that's impossible; you're talking nonsense!"

The ingredient that allows these two opposites to merge into a coherent whole is "bitul," the self-nullification of Judah. The setting aside of his concern for his honor, his own ego, was the catalyst for revealing the ultimate truth. There was the free choice of Tamar, and at the same time, there was G-d controlling the events.

Somehow, this seems to be the key. Making oneself transparent to the will of G-d allows for these two opposites to merge and align. The difference between this Sichah and the previous one is that here, the focus is more on the individual. In the previous Sichah, the focus was on the community as a whole. This recalls the point made in the Talmud (Avoda Zarah, bottom of 4B, top of 5A) as to why two examples of compulsion to sin are given; the sin of the Golden Calf and the sin of King David with Bat Sheva. The Talmud says it was to show that Teshuvah is possible both on the communal level and by the individual.

III

THE JOURNEYS SICHAH

Vol. 18, pages 393–398, paragraphs 5–10

CIRCA 1965

Chapter 33 of Numbers reviews the 42 journeys of the Jewish People from the time they left Egypt until they reached the border of the Land of Israel, 40 years later. The words in parenthesis are my additions.

(Free translation) The 42 journeys of the Jews during their 40 years in the desert are an instruction for everyone. The Medrash (an interpretive teaching of the sages) gives a parable to illustrate what took place. A king had a sick son, so he took the son to a different place to heal him. (The treatment of the son was successful) and as they were returning home, his father began telling him about all the places they had traveled through on the way out. The king said to his son, "here we slept; here we caught cold; here your head ached." In like fashion, G-d said to Moses, "Point out for them all the places where they angered me." Therefore, it says, "These are the journeys of the Children of Israel."

Every soul descends from the highest spiritual level imaginable into a place of the utmost concealment. The purpose of this descent is twofold. First, it is to refine this world, which is likened to a desert. Secondly, it is to enable the soul to reach an even higher level than it was originally at before it underwent the descent. Still, it appears we are talking about two separate concepts; the journeys which appear as exile and darkness, and the goal of elevation that later emerges from the descent.

This bifurcation of the process into descent and elevation only applies when one is actually experiencing the journeys and undergoing the descent. However, once the elevation is actually experienced, the ultimate truth underlying the descent will be revealed. This truth is that the descent is not a different or separate thing from the elevation, but part and parcel of the elevation itself.

It is important to note that the descent and the ascent are along the exact same route. On the way down, the journey appears to be one of concealment, harshness, and darkness. However, on the return trip, it is correctly seen as actually being one of revelation, pleasantness, and illumination.

The key to understanding how this can be is in realizing that the soul is not undertaking the journey alone. The soul is traveling with G-d. Furthermore, G-d is actually escorting the soul during the entire journey. Even more so, the entire journey, and every detail of the journey, is for the benefit of the soul. This being so, it is crystal clear that the descent, in all its outward manifestations, is, at its core, an expression of kindness.

One might still raise a question. It is conceded that the experience of descent as a whole is an expression of kindness, and ultimately uplifting. We are forced to concede this point because the whole process was admittedly set in motion by G-d, and we accept as a basic principle, that G-d is good. Nevertheless, when one sins, it could be argued that an additional descent has been caused, more than was originally built into the system by G-d. Must we concede that even this enhanced aspect of the descent is also for the sake of the subsequent elevation? Furthermore, if we must say that even this is true, perhaps it can be limited to the end result. Can it possibly be that the enhanced descent one caused by their sins, is at its core, part of the ascent?

The answer is, yes, it is. How this can be, is explained at length in the Avram Sichah (the last Sichah that will be discussed), and by the Mitteller Rebbe (the second Chabad Rebbe) in his book, *Toras Chaim*. The foundation for understanding this concept is based on a mystical inter-pretation of the verse in Psalms 66:5: "... an enormous deception has been perpetrated on mankind." This interpretation teaches us that there are times when the power placed at the disposal of the "evil inclination" will overpower the individual and make him or her sin.

However, at this point, when it seems that the matter has been resolved, we must invoke that eternal caveat. All of what has been said does not negate the axiomatic principle that each individual has Free Choice. Everyone has the choice of whether to sin, and rightly deserves the result-ing reward or punishment for the choice that was made.

The reason we still have free choice is as follows. The force from above that causes evil to overpower good is asserted in such a lofty capac-ity that it is not sensed within the person doing the evil act, here, in this lowly physical world. Therefore, the person cannot be said to be compelled, hence, they can still exercise their free choice. This is like the well-known, related concept that G-d's foreknowledge of events does not compel the outcome.

At the end of the day, we must conclude that, yes, even the enhanced descent caused by one's sins, is part of G-d's original intent. G-d intended, through the process of Teshuvah (repentance), that there would be attained the benefit of light that can emerge only against a background of darkness. The end result is that intentional sins are converted to merits.

It comes out that there are two types of descent, which is to say, sin. The first type is likened to those journeys where the presence of G-d is clearly apparent, and there is no doubt that G-d brought the person to the situation. The second type is where G-d's involvement is concealed, and everything seems to be an outcome of the person's free choice. The first case is illustrated by the three journeys leading up to the splitting of the Red Sea, and the second case is illustrated by the remaining journeys during the 40 years in the desert.

The sages say that the first three journeys preceding the splitting of the Red Sea were absolutely necessary. By contrast, the other journeys, starting from the other side of the Red Sea, were a result of choices made to sin.

The explanation is that there are three identifiable areas. There is Egypt (civilization), the first three journeys, and the desert. The second area, the first three journeys (through the "borderlands"), are an interface between civilization and the desert.

In spiritual terms, the desert is a place where G-d is not revealed. The forces of evil are assertive and oppose G-d's will. However, the process that leads to the desert (the first three journeys through the borderlands) was from the beginning designed by G-d. During the first three journeys, G-d is openly leading the people. In the remaining journeys, G-d's involvement is concealed, and it looks like the events that take place are a result of human free choice.

Returning to the Medrash, the first three journeys where G-d's involvement is openly revealed, are described by three expressions. At the first stopover, it says, "we slept" (the king and his son). At the second stop it says, "we were cold." At the third one, it says, "your head ached" (referring only to the son). These three expressions indicate the three active ingredients necessary for there to be Free Choice in a person's service to G-d.

Step One: The soul must descend from its original place where G-d's presence is revealed, into an artificially created arena where G-d's presence is concealed. This is the only way for there to be the possibility of one choosing to act in opposition to G-d's will.

Step Two: Having created this artificial environment insulated from G-d's revealed presence, it became apparent that the pendulum, so to speak, had been allowed to swing too far. As such, there had to be a counter-balancing infusion of G-d's revealed presence to now allow for one to be able to choose to act in accordance with G-d's will.

Step Three: Alas, step two tipped the balance back too far, again, in the other direction. There was no longer the possibility to choose to act against G-d's will. As a result, a further correction was required. This was the granting of the Animal Soul (in the teachings of Chassidus, the power that directly enlivens the body and is motivated by self-interest) the power of intellect. This power of intellect is what allows one to rationalize behavior, that one knows is in opposition to G-d's will.

These three stages are described in the three metaphors used by the Medrash. In the first stage, G-d says, "we slept." The sages understand sleep as 1/60 of death. Thus, when one is asleep, intellect is not active, as when one is awake. This "sleep," which affects both the king (G-d), and his son (the individual), is a metaphor for the creation of the space where G-d's presence is concealed.

In the second stage, the king says, "we experienced cold." Normally, cold is a bad thing. Here, however, it is talking about dissipating the "heat" that was generated by constructing the space where G-d's presence is concealed.

In the third stage, the king says, "there your head ached." This refers to the granting of intellect to the Animal Soul, which allows for the individual to choose to do things that are in opposition to G-d's will.

In conclusion, those descents which appear to result from one's personal choices were in fact intended by G-d to happen from the very beginning. It is just that G-d's involvement in ordering these events is concealed. So, these descents (which we stubbornly insist are a result of one's free choice), are in truth, a result of situations arranged by G-d. Going back to the metaphor of the king and his son; true, the son got sick because of decisions he made of his own free choice. However, in the final analysis, these decisions of the son were part of the entire journey as orchestrated by G-d. Furthermore, the son was supposed to "get sick," so he can then be cured. This is the power of Teshuvah that allows the soul to return to a higher level than from where it originally began its descent into this world. (End of the Rebbe's words).

This Sichah contains a much longer and more detailed discussion of the subject than any of the other references. The reason for this is, that it tries to explain how the two forces, Free Choice and Divine Providence, are able to work side by side. Most other Sichahs simply state the fact as a given without trying to explain how it works. Once again, the Rebbe highlights in the footnotes the "Avram Sichah," in Volume 5, page 65, of Likkutei Sichot, and the long discourse by the Mittler Rebbe from Toras Chaim. This would seem to reinforce the conclusion that these are the Rebbe's "go to" sources on this subject.

Another point that this Sichah makes is that the predominance of Divine Providence applies to all of us, even in our mundane lives. It is not something that is limited to one-time events, or that involve special people. This point is made by using the journeys of the entire people as the starting point of the discussion, events that apply to everyone equally over the course of a lifetime.

Why does the Rebbe want us to know that Divine Providence is the dominant force, and Free Choice is, at best, secondary, and maybe even nothing more than an illusion? On hearing this, the intellect of the Animal Soul (that we were introduced to in this Sichah) perks up and says, "Aha, it's not really my fault if I sin! Let's eat, drink and be merry, and someday we'll do Teshuvah, and everything will be in accord with the divine will!" I am sure the Rebbe does not want this to be the take-away from this Sichah. So, why are we made privy to this subtle insight that can easily be perverted by an ever-vigilant Animal Soul?

I believe the answer is that the Rebbe feels it is critical, in spite of this risk, for everyone to appreciate the unique benefit that can only come as a result of Teshuvah. This provides solace for our own failures. It is not an excuse, but it empowers us to move forward. The words of a Tzadik, once verbalized, and especially after they are committed to being published for all to see, are a "nesinas koach" (an infusion of strength and empowerment). If where I am at is part of G-d's plan, and I am not alone, then I have the ability to redress my failures.

Of course, the failures we see in others are much more obvious. However, they, too, get the benefit of this teaching. Furthermore, now that I am privy to the inner truth, I am less likely to judge them or plaster them with negative labels (mumer, rasha, apikores). They are on the same journey as me. Instead of shunning or condemning them, perhaps they can be encourage along the way.

IV.

THE MILK SICHAH

Vol. 17, page 21, paragraph 8

CIRCA 1976

Chapter 1 of Leviticus discusses details of sacrifices. In connection with bird offerings, verse 15 explains how the blood is applied to the altar, through a squeezing or pressing action. All this is a question of ritual procedure. After this issue is dealt with, the Rebbe shifts to a completely different spiritual plane. The words in parenthesis are my additions.

(Free translation) The question (again) comes up. In the default state, a Jew will not sin. As the Alter Rebbe (the first Chabad Rebbe) explains in Tanya, a Jew does not possess the desire or ability to be separated from G-d. So, when a Jew does in fact sin, it is a result of the "deception" (reference to Psalms 66:5), so to speak, perpetrated on the Jew, by G-d. (Thus, Free Choice is not a true factor in the process). Therefore (since G-d is just and cannot punish someone who was compelled to sin), we say, "Ultimately, no one will be pushed away forever" (reference to Samuel II, 14, 14); ("The No Jew Left Behind," principle). That is, ultimately every Jew will do Teshuvah. If so, why does G-d make Jews go through this process of sinning, to be followed by Teshuvah?

A metaphor for understanding this is found in milk. Upon examining milk for the first time, one sees a substance that was squeezed out of an animal. As a result, the logical conclusion is that this substance is forbidden to eat. It is either a substance that was produced from the blood of the animal (blood being forbidden) or because it is a "limb" of a living animal (it is forbidden to eat a limb of a still living animal). However, Torah surprises us and declares milk to be permissible. More than that, we are told that milk is a symbol for praising the Land of Israel, as in a "land flowing with milk and honey."All this illustrates the principle of "eshapka" (conversion). That is to say, the taking of something that was forbidden and converting it into something permitted, and even praiseworthy.

The same thing applies regarding sin. First the person (is compelled to) sin. This "angers" G-d and calls forth punishment. This punishment is administered for the purpose of getting the Jew to (sooner or later) do Teshuvah. The end result is the suppression, and ultimately, the conversion, of evil into good. It is this which gives G-d the greatest pleasure. (End of the Rebbe's words).

One of the striking things about this Sichah is that up until the last paragraph, there was no hint that the Rebbe was going to discuss the subject of Free Choice. This Sichah was complete before the Rebbe, almost gratuitously, brought the subject up again. I believe this shows a desire of the Rebbe to teach us about this subject time and again, in widely different contexts. The question, again, is why? It is a subtle topic, that ultimately does not get resolved by a definitive answer, and that could, as pointed out above, lead one to not take appropriate responsibility for their actions. Once again, I believe the answer is that the Rebbe wants us to appreciate the greatness of Teshuvah.

On a more positive note, this Sichah shows how punishment fits into the equation. Punishment is not an end for itself. The purpose of punishment is to provide the impetus to do Teshuvah. This helps to answer the sticky question of how G-d can punish people for doing things they were ultimately compelled to do.

However, the analysis is actually more detailed and can be broken down into three steps. The starting point is that no Jew has the capacity to sin. Their spiritual make-up just will not allow for it, despite the challenges of the physical world and the inducements of the yetzer hara (evil inclination).

At this point, G-d intervenes and "stirs the pot." This is the "alilah," the deception, the fraud, perpetrated by G-d himself. Every sin committed by any Jew is a result of this compulsion by G-d! Is there anyone who does not do a double-take on reading this? Yet the Rebbe put it in writing and signed his name to it!

However, in the end, no Jew will be left behind. Everyone will do Teshuvah. So, what has been gained? Are we just back where we started from? If it is all just a wash, then it would be one massive exercise in futility.

Over Passover, I heard that when the "chametz" (the unconsumed leavened products) are "sold" to the non-Jew for the duration of the festival, the bill of sale worked up by the rabbis provides for the buyer, the non-Jew, to realize a profit from the transaction when he sells the chametz back to the rabbi once Passover ends. After all, no one in the real-world buys and sells just to shift merchandise around. There must be a profit.

So too, in our relationship between G-d and every Jew. At the end of the day, there is a profit for the Jew and a profit for G-d. The soul emerges at a much higher level from where it started, while G-d, for his part, experiences unquantifiable pleasure when the soul returns victorious. From G-d's perspective, a "chidush" (something new) has been achieved, and his infinite "boredom" (or his boredom at being unchangingly infinite) has somehow been alleviated.

V.

THE 'KORACH' SICHAH

Vol. 8, page 118, paragraph 7

CIRCA 1958 & 1964

Chapter 16 of Numbers describes the rebellion of Korach against the authority of Moses and the priesthood headed by Aaron, the brother of Moses. The words in parenthesis are my additions.

(Free translation) There is a parallel between the creation of the firmament on the second day of creation, and the rebellion fomented by Korach. The firmament was created to make a separation between the upper and lower waters. However, this separation was only a prelude to the connection between the upper and lower realms which was completed on the third day of creation.

In a similar vein is the separation that was caused by Korach. The reason G-d made Korach's rebellion happen was in order to reaffirm and strengthen the connection between the priesthood and the people at large.

(The Rebbe refers the reader to footnote 36, and says look at the "Avram" Sichah, which will be the last Sichah discussed. In the body of the footnote, the Rebbe states): Also, the descents that occur in the world because of our sins, since they are scripted in accord with G-d's direction, are for the purpose of leading to the elevation that follows the sin. Nevertheless, this does not negate Free Choice, because G-d's writing the script (Hashgachah) does not compel our actions. (End of the Rebbe's words).

This Sichah does not offer explanations; it just tells us that G-d made Korach's rebellion happen. At the same time, the Rebbe tells us that this does not negate the free choice of those involved. Korach and those that joined him still had free choice. We are left to ponder how this might work.

The problem in discussing the issue in this context is the fact that in the aftermath of Korach's rebellion, people actually die. It is not just that "punishment" was administered to pressure the people involved to do Teshuvah. The same question arises in connection with the incident of the Golden Calf. At the end of the day, a lot of people died. Some were killed outright by the Levites, some died by being forced to drink from the water with the ashes of the Golden Calf, and some were killed in the plague sent by G-d.

If Free Choice is ultimately an illusion, and the people involved were compelled to sin, how can this outcome be justified, or even make sense? On the other hand, if we have free choice, what does the Rebbe mean when he says, "G-d made Korach's rebellion happen"? How can both statements be true?

The solution to this conundrum is that there is no solution. Meaning, a solution that satisfies our human desire for everything to make sense on our finite level of understanding. However, a new insight does emerge. Furthermore, we can no longer be so sure that Korach is the consummate villain. After all, the entire Torah portion is named after him.

VI.
THE COUNTING THE OMER SICHAH

Vol. 3, page 976, footnote 19

CIRCA 1960

Chapter 9 of Leviticus describes the eighth day of the installation rites of Aaron and his sons as priests. The Rebbe explains the connection of these events to the Counting of the Omer, the 49 days between Passover and the giving of the Torah at Mt. Sinai. However, the real "Sunday Punch" is delivered in Footnote 19; total lagniappe!

(Free translation) From the day we left Egypt, we have been progressing, individually and collectively, in going out of our boundaries and limitations. From a distance, it appears to uniformly consist of climbing higher and higher.

(Footnote 19) Over the course of time, there have been changes in circumstances, consisting of many ups and downs. As the verse states, "seven times the righteous one falls and then rises." Every falling is for the sake of the rising that follows. Furthermore, this rhythm of rising and falling is required. It cannot be any other way.

It has been explained elsewhere at length that between every stage in this upward progression, there must be an intervening state of nullification. This principle also applies when the movement is in a downward direction. In each descent from level to level, there must be a stage of non-existence intervening between each level of existence.

As to the upward progression, since each descent is a necessary prelude to attaining the next higher level, this descent is not a true descent. It is actually part of the subsequent higher level that has been attained. The reason for this is rooted in G-d's intent in creating the world. Creation is a downward directional process. Once the downward progression was completed, and a physical world created, the direction of movement was reversed to one of a constant upward progression. Since this was G-d's intent prior to implementing the creative process, it must be that this is the way it actually plays out. After all, at the time of the formation of G-d's intent, no forces of opposition, however subtle or refined, existed. Therefore, once the lowest level at the end of the descent was reached, our physical world, there is no other option but for the process of ascent to begin and to continue unabated.

Therefore, we must say, that personal free choice, merely touches on the fringes of reality. It has no impact on the ultimate destiny of creation. Creation is always and exclusively headed in an upward direction. This comports with the intent behind creation before it was created in actuality.

Carried to the next logical level, the same dynamic applies to everyone. Each individual is constantly progressing to a higher level.

So, the only impact on the system that a person has through the exercise of their free choice is on the speed and direction in attaining the goal. As to speed, the sages have said, if we merit, G-d will hasten the Redemption. If we do not merit, G-d will bring it in its appointed time. In regard to direction, this means one of two choices, reminiscent of the difference between the service of a Tzadik (a perfectly righteous person), and a Baal Teshuvah (a person who sinned and has repented).

The first choice (that of the Baal Teshuvah) involves choosing to sin, thus infusing evil into the system. This direction will then require Teshuvah in order to counteract the evil. This will have the benefit of leading to an ultimate victory where evil is actively engaged, suppressed, and ultimately converted to good. In this dynamic, the individual who sins still deserves punishment, because the choice to sin was not made with the lofty intent of accomplishing this ultimate victory.

The second choice (that of the Tzadik) is to only go upward. There is a complete rejection of evil that avoids any backsliding whatsoever. Since no evil was chosen, there is no need for Teshuvah. The journey is short and direct.

The point is that either way is consistent with G-d's original will in creating the world. A person's choices merely affect whether the journey is long or short, direct, or circuitous. In choosing to sin, one incurs punishment, but having engaged evil along the way, attains a more complete victory. In choosing not to sin, one avoids punishment and has a quick and direct journey. But having bypassed evil, one has a less complete victory. (End of the Rebbe's words).

This Sichah is dated 1960. At the end of footnote 19 is an additional footnote which tells us that the source of the material just presented is from comments of the Rebbe going back to 1952 at the time of the passing of the Rebbe's brother. The Rebbe became the Rebbe of Chabad in 1951, so these thoughts were publicized very early in the Rebbe's tenure as the Rebbe.

Once again, the discussion of free choice was injected here almost gratuitously, in a lengthy footnote. It is not necessary for the completeness of the Sichah in which it is found.

However, besides just broaching the subject yet again, the Rebbe provides new insights. He shows how Free Choice truly can be real and not just an illusion of reality. The key is that Free Choice only comes into play in the fine tuning of the system. This is the critical point, and it applies to the world as a whole, and, even more intriguing, to the life of every individual.

I have devised a metaphor to illustrate this point based on my own readings and from watching WWII movies. During World War II, American bombers flying missions over Germany took off from their base, drop their bombs on their target, and then flew back home. For the mission as a whole, the planes were controlled by the pilot. As the planes approached their target, each pilot would transfer control of the plane to their bombardier who could make whatever adjustments were needed in the flight of the plane so that the bombs could be dropped with as much precision as possible. Once the bombs were dropped, the pilot would resume control of the plane for the trip home.

When it comes to a person's life, G-d (the pilot) has it all mapped out from start to finish. At critical junctures when choices must be made, G-d releases the controls to the person for the exercise of free choice. If the person makes the right choices, the mission (the person's life) proceeds smoothly to its ultimate conclusion. If the person makes the wrong choices, some sort of rectification will be required. In the bomber analogy, if the bombardier fails to drop his bombs, for whatever reason, the pilot is going to have to circle back for another attempt at the target or fly home with the knowledge that another mission to the same target is going to have to be planned. The circling back option is like doing Teshuvah, where the person gets a second chance to make up for an earlier failure. The second option of flying a whole new mission is perhaps where the concept of reincarnation comes in. Failure in one lifetime means the soul comes down again (and perhaps again) for a repeat mission.

The Rebbe said all this as part of his reflections on the life of his brother. I think the significance of this cannot be overstated. People had questions. In short, the Rebbe's brother was not the Rebbe, not in his level of learning or in his level of religious commitment. So, the Rebbe says, "Don't draw conclusions." Every life has a G-dly plan and its unique trajectory.

Another point that is addressed is that of punishment. A person can be justly punished for their sins, since it is certain that the sins were not committed with the lofty intent of facilitating G-d's plan. If the person were truly compelled, or the action was taken with the lofty intent of elevating the evil, then there would be no punishment.

Another element that is mentioned is the ingredient of "bittul" (self-nullification). In progressing from one level to another, whether going up or down, a state of bittul must be experienced in order to make the transition. We previously saw in the Tamar Sichah that the bittul of Judah was needed for a satisfactory resolution of the conflict between Free Choice and Divine Providence. Perhaps this is a recurring theme and a key to our understanding of the issue.

In positing that bittul is the key, this is helpful but also frustrating. As long as we are alive, I believe that none of us (with the exception of rare tzadikim, as described in Tanya) will ever attain true bittul. This may explain why we cannot truly resolve the conundrum. However, we can on an intellectual level appreciate that with real and complete bittul, Free Choice and Divine Providence would become aligned, and the contradiction between them operating at the same time would disappear. So, while we cannot understand the solution, we can understand that there is a solution.

VII

THE MIXED MULTITUDE AND GOLDEN CALF SICHAH

Vol. 16, page 412, paragraph 8

CIRCA 1964, 1971, & 1976

Chapter 33 of Exodus begins with a description of how Moses continued to deal with the people who worshipped the Golden Calf, particularly members of the Mixed Multitude. The words in parenthesis are my additions.

[Free translation] The ultimate rectification of the sin of the golden calf is expressed in the treatment of the Mixed Multitude. (Earlier in the Sichah, the Rebbe explained that those people from the Mixed Multitude who worshiped the Golden Calf but did not receive a warning beforehand and did not have witnesses against them, not only survived but were enhanced and elevated through doing Teshuvah. In contrast, those who were born Jews, in the same legal situation, were tested with water and ashes of the ground up Golden Calf, like "sotahs" [unfaithful wives], and died.)

This can be understood by examining the statement of the sages: "The Jews (ostensibly including the Mixed Multitude) at that time were not capable of doing such a thing (i.e. worshipping the Golden Calf). The entire episode was a product of a 'decree from G-d', the purpose of which was to provide a precedent for future generations who would want to do Teshuvah." (Footnote 28 of the Sichah provides the source citations).

This precedent was not just for future generations. It was also for the benefit of the people of that generation, so that they, too, should get the benefit that comes from Teshuvah. A unique characteristic of Teshuvah is that one cannot choose this path at the outset. If one plans to sin, and then repent, the option of repentance is withheld from them. It is only after one sins, that they are given the opportunity, and thus the corresponding obligation, to do Teshuvah.

Nevertheless, there is greater value in the service of one who does Teshuvah over the service of a completely righteous individual who never sinned. This is why the sages say, "The place where one who repents stands, is at a level that the completely righteous cannot attain." (Footnote 31 of the Sichah provides the source citations).

For this reason, G-d intervened and gave the "evil inclination" the upper hand over people who had experienced the unprecedented revelations at the giving of the Torah. As they were, following such revelations, they were not capable of sinning. They had complete control over any inclination to sin. As a result, G-d had to intervene and cause them to sin so they could obtain the benefit that comes from sinning, followed by Teshuvah. (End of the Rebbe's words).

This Sichah does not explore the logic behind how Free Choice and Divine Providence can coexist. It also does not address the troubling fact, noted earlier, that people were put to death for an act they were compelled to do. What it does provide is a reason for why G-d compels or forces someone to sin. The reason is that G-d prefers the service of a Baal Teshuvah (one who repents after sinning) over the service of a Tzadik (a completely righteous individual).

This point is made so many times in the Sichahs of the Rebbe that its impact might be overlooked. However, we really ought to take note. The Rebbe is constantly emphasizing that <u>we</u> are where it is at. For all our ups and downs, it is our service that means the most to G-d, not the service of Tzadikim (including the Rebbe, himself).

The reason for this preference has been previously mentioned. It is that the Baal Teshuvah engages, suppresses, and ultimately converts evil to holiness. By doing so, he or she elevates sparks of holiness that the Tzadik never confronts.

If we employ the metaphor of a military battle, we are the frontline soldiers, while the Tzadik is the general. This general is normally stationed in the rear, issuing commands far removed from the frontline fighting. The general may have the victory attached to his name in the history books, but it is the soldiers under his command that win or lose the battle.

So, another myth is debunked. We might want to curb our worship of the "tzadikim" among us (the rabbis, the religious-school teachers, the young (and not so young) men in Kollel). This includes the Rebbe himself, who probably "rolled his eyes" at the constant adulation he received whenever he walked into a room or walked down the street. Of course, we love and respect all the above for all they do for us, but we need to take more pride in our role as the ones that confront the stiffest challenges of the world head on.

This Sichah also tells us about the relationship between Moses and the Mixed Multitude. Even G-d refers to them "crossly" as the people that you, Moses, brought out of the land of Egypt. It was your idea, says G-d, to allow them to accompany the biological descendants of the patriarchs through the Red Sea, and to experience the revelation at Mt. Sinai. When they relapsed back into their old ways and incited "the Children of Israel" to sin through the Golden Calf, the blame is laid at Moses' feet.

After the revelation of Mt. Sinai, when a general conversion of the entire people is understood to have taken place, there is maintained a distinction between members of the twelve tribes and the Mixed Multitude. The most obvious manifestation of this divide is the fact that the Mixed Multitude were forced to travel "at the back of the bus," so to speak, outside of the Clouds of Glory. When the nation halted in their journeys, people from the Mixed Multitude were not allowed to set up camp with the rest of the Tribes.

Nevertheless, the Rebbe points out that one of the reasons Moses died in the desert was to be there to see to the ultimate refinement of those members of the Mixed Multitude that also died in the desert (footnote 26). Moses was willing to endure the disapproval of the rest of the nation, and even G-d, in exchange for harnessing the potential he saw concealed in these people. An obvious parallel can be drawn from this to the way the Rebbe chose to relate to non-observant Jews of his generation. The Rebbe spent his entire tenure as Rebbe in America, and ultimately, just like Moses, was buried outside of Israel among the people he cared about most.

VIII

THE ELIEZER SICHAH

Vol. 25, page 103, paragraphs 6–8

CIRCA 1982 & 1984

Chapter 24, verse 4 of Genesis begins the episode of Abraham sending his servant, Eliezer, back to Abraham's former home, in Charan, to find a wife for Isaac. The words in parenthesis are my additions.

(Free translation) How can Abraham guarantee Eliezer that he will be successful in convincing Rivka (Rebecca) to come back with him to marry Isaac? It seems to ignore the very real possibility that she might exercise her free choice and refuse to go with him.

However, this is the power behind the statement that, "G-d will send His angel before you." This is a power that stems from a place that "precedes" and is "higher" than human effort. As such, an emanation from this level will be successfully revealed below in our world. It is not dependent on the effort of people to bring it to fruition. Nor can human will in opposition to this emanation prevent its occurrence.

So, even though there is Free Choice, and thus the possibility Rivka will reject Eliezer's petition, nevertheless it is certain that G-d's will is going to prevail; there will be a woman who will agree to go with Eliezer (back to Israel and marry Isaac).

Now, the sages have said, "Better are the (casual) words of the servants of the patriarchs, than the teachings of their descendants (the sages of the

Torah)." One of the teachings of the sages is "Everything is in the hands of heaven, except the fear of heaven." This means, in matters of learning Torah and keeping the Commandments, a person is not deprived of Free Choice.

However, regarding the mission of Eliezer, it says, "G-d will send his angel before you," in a fashion that will guarantee your success, notwithstanding the possible opposition of human free choice. The success is guaranteed from above even when it confronts the principle of Free Choice. When such a confrontation occurs, Free Choice gives way to Divine Providence.

To obtain this result, two conditions must be met. Number one, a person must be a "servant of the patriarchs." They exist only to serve their master. Secondly, one must realize they cannot rely on their own strengths but must pray to G-d for the strength to succeed.

All this is summarized in the legal ruling of the Rambam (Maimonides). "The concept of free choice is a fundamental belief, and the support for Torah and its Commandments. Still and all, Torah itself already promised us that in the end, Israel will do Teshuvah, which will result in Israel's immediate redemption." (End of the Rebbe's words).

This Sichah posits the reality of both Free Choice and Divine Providence. When there is a conflict between the two, however, Divine Providence wins out. The reason for this is that Divine Providence emanates from a higher level in G-d's essence. Thus, when the two forces come into conflict with each other, Divine Providence will always trump Free Choice.

The Rambam couched the discussion in legal terms. Free choice is real and necessary, but at the same time, G-d has already determined that Israel will ultimately do Teshuvah. This statement can easily be glossed over and leave us unimpressed. I believe the Rebbe is saying, "Stop and think what the Rambam just said!" There is Free Choice when it comes to Torah and Mitzvahs, and there is, at the same time, the guarantee that Israel (that is, every Jew) will do teshuvah. The course and goal have been predetermined, but G-d allows for a certain amount of "play" in the system through human free choice along the way.

Another point that emerges in the Sichah that we have not seen before is that sometimes Free Choice is cast as the "villain" in this dynamic.

We like to think of Free Choice as our G-d-given right and vehemently object to any undercutting of what we see as a fundamental prerogative. However, in the context of this Sichah, we see that Free Choice is the cause of the problem, and Eliezer prays that G-d will assert Himself and make sure that events play out consistent with His will.

Finally, once again, "bittul" comes into play as the necessary ingredient to merit G-d's intervention. To tap into the higher level of reality we call Divine Providence, we need bittul, the expression of self-nullification, previously discussed. If we can muster the requisite level of bittul, and pray with appropriate intent, we may merit to receive this high level of revelation that steamrolls all opposition to G-d's will that is manifested through human machinations.

IX.

THE MIRIAM
SICHAH

Vol. 18, page 138, paragraph 9

CIRCA 1965

Chapter 12, verse 15 of Numbers describes the seven-day confinement of Miriam outside the camp, after she was stricken with tzara'at (leprosy) for criticizing Moses for separating from his wife. The verse states that the people did not travel until her return to the camp. The words in parenthesis are my additions.

(Free translation) It was discussed earlier in this Sichah, the difference between the Mishnah and Rashi. The Mishnah says, "Therefore, Israel waited for her" (for Miriam to be healed from her leprosy before they resumed their travel). The Mishnah also recognizes that the immediate cause for Israel not traveling was the fact G-d did not raise the cloud (the signal for the people to break camp). The Mishnah, however, wants to emphasize that there was also significance in the people wanting to wait for Miriam's recovery.

Rashi deviated from the Mishnah and attributed the people waiting for Miriam entirely to G-d. He writes, "This honor (of the people waiting for her) was bestowed on her from G-d." Rashi agrees that the people also wanted to wait for her, but the emphasis is that what really counted was G-d's desire to honor her.

The inner reason for the difference in approach between the Mishnah and Rashi is as follows. The sages (from the era of the Mishhah) have said, "Everything is in the hands of heaven, except the fear of heaven." For this reason, the Mishnah finds it difficult to accept that this good deed, of waiting for Miriam, only happened because G-d imposed His will, and not because this was the will of the people. According to the Mishnah, the fact that the cloud remained anchored in place was a result of, and in response to, the people's desire to wait for her. The input of the people was a significant factor in determining whether to wait for her.

Rashi looks at it differently. Even conceding that the people also wanted to wait for her, it would be difficult to argue that this journey differed from all the other journeys, all of which were initiated solely in accordance with G-d's will.

On a deeper level, we can say that Rashi is trying to teach us the ultimate truth, and the most profound way to understand the dynamic. That is, decisions (for good or bad) that we have always been taught (by the sages of the Mishnah) were given over to one's exercise of Free Choice, also originate from above, from higher than human free choice. They come from a level that can be labeled, "the hands of heaven." Applying this understanding to the case of Miriam, the desire of the people to honor Miriam and wait for her, ultimately came about because of a directive from G-d.

The Mishnah, on the other hand, teaches Torah on a more basic, revealed level. At this level of teaching, it is not openly taught that human actions are directed from above. To do so would present a contradiction to the principle of Free Choice. The Mishnah wanted to emphasize the paramount importance of personal effort in serving G-d. (End of the Rebbe's words).

This Sichah presents the idea of approaching the issue of the conflict between Free Choice and Divine Providence as a function of the times. The ultimate truth has always been the same. The only issue was how much was appropriate to reveal in earlier times. (A similar idea is explained regarding the theme of the month of Tamuz; Likkutei Sichot, Vol. 18, paragraph 5, page 314).

Back in the days of the Mishnah, people, in general, were not that removed from being constantly connected to G-d. As such, they could be relied on to rectify whatever failings they experienced by dint of their own effort. As time went on, and the darkness of exile increased, more emphasis needed to be put on G-d's involvement in the process of getting people to do Teshuvah. This is reflected in Rashi hinting at this truth in his time (Rashi died in 1105 CE). The Rebbe in his time decided that the time had come to openly declare that the masquerade is over. Everything comes from G-d, even matters pertaining to "the fear of heaven" (page 140 of the Sichah).

Still, we can ask, why now? Why not just stick with the teaching of the Mishnah that has worked well enough all through the ages and up to the present time? I think the Rebbe's answer would be that the challenges of the times mandate it. The Sichah is about Miriam as she is afflicted with tzara'at (leprosy if you will). This is a stringent level of impurity and requires banishment from all the camps. A person on such a low level will find it very hard to generate on their own the drive to do Teshuvah. The difficulty is only compounded when the challenges and the spiritual darkness of the present times are added to the mix.

So, I think what the Rebbe is doing is reminding us that in the end, everyone will do Teshuvah. G-d will not leave anyone behind. You are not on your own, so do not be daunted by the challenge. Since this is the case, why wait? Do it now and I am here to help. There will come a time when I will not be here in person, but my books are here. Open them up and learn, get inspired, and do Teshuvah. Now!

X.

THE AVRAM SICHAH

Vol. 5, page 65, end of paragraph 10

CIRCA 1953, 1961, & 1965

Chapter 12, verse 10 of Genesis describes Avram's descent to Egypt. He had just arrived in Israel on G-d's command, and now, following a famine, was forced to seek refuge in Egypt. The words in parenthesis are my additions.

(Free translation) When one commits an actual sin (not like the "sins" of the patriarchs), this act is categorically against G-d's will. Still, one needs to realize, that on the innermost level, they are still acting in accord with G-d's plan. Even at the time of the commission of the sin, they are still in the process of progressing upward from level to level.

(Having stated this fact, the Rebbe offers a "brief" explanation of how this works)

One of our fundamental beliefs is that G-d has sole control over the conduct of the world. Any other powers, spiritual or physical, that seem to exert influence over events, are merely like an axe in the hand of the woodsman. To believe anything short of this would be in contradiction to our belief in the unity of G-d.

This principle applies with equal force to human decisions and actions. This includes matters involving Torah and its Commandments, the one area where we also say that people are given Free Choice. Even in this area, all our actions and decisions are dictated according to Divine Providence and are in accord with G-d's will.

The difference is that G-d has an "inner" will and an "outer" will. His inner will is expressed in the Torah and its Commandments. His outer will is that a world should exist in all its myriad details. The world also has an "inner" expression and an "outer" expression. The inner expression is to fulfill G-d's will, as expressed in the Torah and its Commandments. The outer expression is simply to be a physical world. G-d's outer will is "closer" to the outer expression of the world. Because of this "proximity," the outer expressions of the world "feel" the influence of G-d's outer will, and thus, are forced to act in accord with this aspect of His will. On the other hand, those matters related to Torah and its Commandments, which are G-d's inner will, are "separated" from the inner expression of the world, which is the desire to fulfill G-d's will in matters related to Torah and its Commandments. Because of this "separation," G-d's inner will is not consciously sensed by people charged with fulfilling the inner expression of the worlds. Thus, in matters of Torah and its Commandments, no one is compelled, and all decisions are a matter of Free Choice.

Furthermore, this matter of Free Choice in connection with Torah and its Commandments, which is such a fundamental principle, is wholeheartedly true, and not just a matter of people *thinking* they have free choice, because the Will controlling them is concealed. (Footnote 71).

What emerges from the above presentation is as follows. There are descents in the world at large, and on an individual scale, that were caused by one's actions and because of one's Free Choice. At the same time, such decisions and actions are also in accord with G-d's will, what we are calling Divine Providence. As such, they are part of G-d's plan, and these descents are part of the ultimate goal that the world and the people involved in it be elevated.

Another way of saying it is, that a sinful action is certainly the opposite of what G-d wants. At the same time, the descent, the damage, to the world and to the individual caused by the sin is not something that conflicts with G-d's will. It is not a true or permanent descent. It is a part, a step, in the resulting elevation that emerges at the end of the process.

There is a lesson in all of this for everyone. In whatever situation you find yourself, no matter how degraded and miserable, even when you must admit it is your own fault, because of your decisions in choosing to do evil, still you should never give up and think all is lost. The reason for this optimism is that the situation, in addition to being a result of your free choice, was at the same time directed from above. G-d arranged the events so that through Teshuvah you should reach a much higher spiritual level than you could otherwise have attained. This superior state results from your having refined those sparks of holiness that are found in your intentional sins which have now been converted into merits. Such merits, that are a result of this conversion process, are of a higher quality than the merits of Tzadikim (those completely righteous individuals who never sinned in the first place). (End of the Rebbe's words).

This is one of the earliest Sichahs on the subject. Many of the later Sichahs refer to this Sichah. The Rebbe states the basic principle that both Free Choice and Divine Providence are immutable realities in our lives. He then offers his most complete attempt to explain how they can both simultaneously exist.

The Rebbe uses deceptively simple terminology to explain the paradox. His use of the terms "inner" will, "outer" will, "separate," and "close" sound unsophisticated and too simplistic to constitute a serious explanation of such a perplexing phenomenon. If someone with a PhD in philosophy were to tackle the problem, they would use much more technical and sophisticated terminology that would leave us impressed, if totally in the dark. The Rebbe, on the other hand, is trying to communicate to the average person who is not trained in philosophy, or familiar with the philosophers' specialized vocabulary.

Now, someone who is not a die-hard fan of the Rebbe might say: "What has the Rebbe accomplished? He has not provided any clear-cut answers, and in fact, has left us even more confused! Better to have left matters the way the Mishnah put it, that "everything is in the hands of

37

heaven except the fear of heaven." We agree that G-d is in charge of every-thing else but has carved out a space in matters pertaining to Torah and Mitzvahs where he has intentionally relinquished control."

The problem, as I see it, is that the "old" approach impinges on the absolute unity of G-d. As such, it may not express the <u>ultimate</u> truth. It also has its own internal problems. Reward and punishment should follow the script, but we see that the righteous suffer and the wicked often prosper. Furthermore, G-d is now let off the hook. We can blame the wickedness of other people, or ourselves, when things go "wrong." Under the Rebbe's dynamic, <u>everything</u> comes back to G-d. The buck stops there. I prefer the Rebbe's approach. When there are unanswerable questions, I would rather leave them for G-d to answer.

So, I think the point is as follows. One should not think of Free Choice and Divine Providence as mutually exclusive forces. Both can exist side by side, without one cancelling out the other. Previously, I saw these two con-cepts as butting heads, with Divine Providence dominating Free Choice. Now, it is more like two ships passing in the night with both remaining on course in their full integrity. Questions remain as to how this can be, but it seems plausible to accept it as true. Ultimately, the real point is the lesson of optimism to be drawn from the discussion. In a nutshell, the Rebbe is reminding us that G-d runs the world, which is to say, the whole world.

CONCLUSIONS AND PERSONAL THOUGHTS

The study of the subject has been completed. The Rebbe's words have been gathered, translated, and put in some semblance of an order. The last thing I want to do is come across as preaching or pretending to be The Expert on the subject. Nevertheless, I will share some insights on what we have learned with the intent being to provoke further thought and discussion on the topic.

A starting point would be to point out that the Rebbe became the leader of Chabad in 1951. His entire tenure as Rebbe was served in America. He never left the US once he arrived. In fact, he hardly ever left New York City. After his passing, he was buried in America (as opposed to being transported to Israel). So, even though the Rebbe preferred to speak in Yiddish, and looked like a Jew from the "Old County," his message, to a large extent, was for American Jews.

The Rebbe could have turned inward, circled the wagons so to speak, and focused on the remnants of European Jews who survived WWII. The Rebbe chose not to do so. Instead of looking inward, the Rebbe turned outward and demanded that his followers do the same. The mission was to unlock the untapped potential contained in every Jew with a special focus on assimilated American Jews.

In light of this backdrop, the Rebbe's views on Free Choice, Divine Providence, and Teshuvah make sense. The vast majority of American Jews were no longer observant. They could be written off as sinners who chose to abandon their faith. The other choice was to view this demographic picture as planned by G-d. G-d arranged for a vast sea of potential Baal

Teshuvahs. Eventually, every one of them will do Teshuvah. The Rebbe saw it as his mission to be proactive and hasten the process.

The Rebbe saw every such Jew as a diamond in the rough, merely waiting for their potential to be unlocked. Every individual was where they were and at their level of observance because that was where G-d led them to be. If such a person could be inspired to make a change to a more observant lifestyle, negative aspects of that person's life would be converted to good. The release of spiritual energy would be awesome and unprecedented.

Furthermore, the attitude toward such a person would be informed by this understanding. The potential Baal Teshuvah was viewed by the Rebbe with utmost respect. They were in their present situation because G-d "personally" led them to such a level. Secondly, if such a person did Teshuvah, they would attain a higher level than those who inspired them, including the Rebbe, himself! No doubt, the Rebbe wanted his followers to share his mindset on this point as they implemented the Rebbe's program. No one condescends to a diamond, however rough or unpolished it might be.

Even more important is the attitude the potential Baal Teshuvah should have toward himself or herself. Bitterness over a state of affairs might be appropriate. However, feelings of guilt, self-loathing, or hopelessness should be emphatically pushed away. Everyone should realize they were brought to their present situation by the "personal" direction of G-d. As such, it is within their capacity to convert and elevate all negativity into positive energy.

This applies equally to someone considering for the first time adopting a more observant lifestyle, as well as someone who was raised observant but left the fold to explore other lifestyles. A diamond is not intimidated by the fact that its brilliance is covered up by extraneous materials.

This attitude would also help a parent cope with the situation where a child abandoned an observant lifestyle. The parent would naturally experience feelings ranging from guilt, anger, embarrassment, confusion, and sorrow. The Rebbe's approach provides hope and peace of mind. The path the child took is part of G-d's plan. No child will be left behind. Sooner or later, everyone will do Teshuvah.

Another realization emerges from the Rebbe's approach to sin. Sins are a reservoir of spiritual energy. I do not need or want anyone to take on my sins or expunge them for me. To do so is plundering a personal resource. I understand that sins are actions taken in opposition to G-d's will, but I have no fear of them. They are a reservoir of energy waiting to be transformed into merits.

This underlying attitude sheds light on the Rebbe's personal behavior of standing tirelessly for hours as all kinds of Jews would file past him to receive a dollar, a piece of cake, a matzah, or a small plastic cup of wine, depending on the occasion. It seems the Rebbe loved gazing at diamonds.

So, the discussion comes full circle. This project was not a book about the Rebbe; it is about a teaching of the Rebbe. However, the Rebbe at his core was a teacher. So, by learning a teaching of the Rebbe, one finds out more about the Rebbe than they would learn by reading his biography.

It seems to me that the crucial point is whether one trusts the Rebbe to be their spiritual guide. If they do, this teaching provides a foundation on which one can ground their entire life. I trust the Rebbe, but it was a result of a process that developed over a period of time. It is not based on posters or slogans, fantastic claims, or stories of miracles performed. It is based on a personal relationship with the Rebbe that was forged by learning his Sichahs. It is as simple as that, taking a book off the shelf and reading or having someone else read to you. Voila, a personal chavrusah (a one-on-one study session) with the Rebbe. This activity, over time, led me to conclude that the Rebbe was the embodiment of Torah; nothing more, nothing less.

I would not confer upon myself the title of "chasid." When people point to me and say, "He's a chasid of the Lubavitcher Rebbe," I squirm in discomfort. The Rebbe has identified various levels from among those who try to connect to him. There are "chassidim," there are those who are "bound" to him, and those "who follow in his wake." The Rebbe took an interest in me as an American Jew going with the flow. I responded by studying his works. He further responded by giving me the knowledge, understanding and insights to live my life with confidence and security. It does not matter if there are challenges and upheavals. It does not matter that other observant Jews sometimes disappoint and act badly. That is not a valid excuse for giving up or succumbing to temptation. The teachings of the Rebbe remain a constant.

ACKNOWLEDGEMENT

My journey started in 1978 when I was a third-year law student at the University of Missouri, Columbia. I met Dr. Levi Reiter and his wife, and Rabbi Yosef Yitzhak (then known as "Icky") Posner and his wife, one late Friday night at the Hillel House, on campus. After that, I spent many days and nights in their homes in Kansas City, Missouri, experiencing and learning about a new and fascinating version of Judaism.

From there, I moved on to yeshivah in Morristown, New Jersey. I spent two years there from mid-1979 to mid-1981. It is impossible to encapsulate that experience in a few lines, so I will simply thank the extraordinary Hancholah (teaching staff) as a whole, along with my fellow students.

After getting married in June of 1981, we moved back to St. Louis, Missouri. Rabbi Yosef Landa is the head Shaliach (Chabad representative) in St. Louis. I have known him for over 40 years. He is the one who encouraged me to complete this project.

For many years after leaving yeshivah, I was intimidated by Yiddish. This created a real barrier to connecting with the Rebbe. Then I came across an opera by Mozart called <u>The Magic Flute</u>. Papageno and the Queen of the Night sing some catchy tunes (albeit in German). Soon, I realized I could understand what they were saying (it *sounded* like they were singing in Yiddish). Well, if I could understand them, with practice, I should be able to learn a Sichah of the Rebbe in Yiddish. And so it went. I wonder what the rabbis at Morristown would think of that as a learning tool for students struggling with Yiddish.

Finally, I dedicate this project to my family; past, present, and especially the future, including my wife's side of the family. Maybe a grandchild or great-grandchild will one day pick up this book and like his Zeide say, "I goes to fight mit Rebbe'n!" (the Rebbe).

HC